II

1

204

Introduction

In 2001, two researchers in New York studied how long people look at works of art. They found that the average time spent viewing was 27,2 seconds. They concluded that a museum visit is "not characterised by long looks at a few works of art; it is characterised by brief looks at many works of art."

It is strange, then, to think that people can be so affected by works of art that they have barely observed. But perhaps this is the true purpose of the viewer. To look at all things and still feel moved by them.

That is my feeling when I read the century of haikus in Massimo Papini's *from the hinted deserts*. I invite you to go through this collection of poems the same way you would browse a museum.

III

Read each line as if it were a thick brushstroke on a painting, or a smoothened form on a sculpture.
And leave with satisfaction.

Amadeus Redha

To everyone
you used to hate.

1

from the hinted deserts

1/100

Aprils of the soul:
too many reasons to hide
under the bluest sky.

2/100

Reading my own flocks
in a continuum of joy
and fearful nonsense.

3/100

Time for warmer wars
against visions I belonged
and estranged sunsets.

4/100

Luxury of buds
in the decadence of May
too unsure to be.

5/100

Mistaken for gods
over the chocking wonder
of a calm morning.

6/100

The punk rock of doves
cornered to concrete comfort
speaking spring fluently.

7/100

A dance of new blood
after the stillest rainstorm
of a packed summer.

8/100

Beauty and misuse
of that city of thunders
dead poets would call love.

9/100

Like a rolling stone
I calmly slit my feelings
on my new way out.

10/100

Memorial cold shores
joining the shredded skylines
in our unshared dreams.

11/100

One night on a coach
to count all the warm bodies
between me and me.

12/100

Weaponised rainbows
and birds over a future
we can't justify.

13/100

Hail to whatever
while gently unravelling
a last minute void.

14/100

Hard as new ideas
the vision of whiter clouds
spraining my surprise.

15/100

See through my fingers
tragedies of new blossoms
against the timeline.

16/100

As long as it takes
to domesticate the rain
I sit on my soul.

17/100

Instant of fireflies
in a more speechless dialogue
that tackles the night.

18/100

White sand in my thoughts
piles of leaves from dead worlds
and winter again.

19/100

Petals are hammers
in inhumane factories
that produce the days.

20/100

I fix the abstract
of inexperienced Mondays
tickling my diary.

21/100

Forbidden sunsets
elegy of a present
where seasons still clash.

22/100

New old perspectives
on my blossoming free fall
that connects two holes.

23/100

I forgave winters
for all the missing white swans
and the smell of hope.

24/100

We all are nothing
and nothing is just a word
but words can hurt too.

25/100

Misunderstanding
the essence of your escape
from a sleepless dawn.

26/100

Flawless imaging
of all my hinted deserts
and eyes wide shut.

27/100

Astonished abysses
on the tray of our true love
looked like joy to me.

28/100

Horizons behind
each and every goodbye
to the last of us.

29/100

Deeply in my mind
mornings over troubled oceans
wounding the instants.

30/100

Not too abstractly
we love struggling to rejoice
at our own failures.

31/100

From my soft castle
I complete the infinite
of five more minutes.

32/100

Explosions of void
give rhythm to my diamond night
at a faster pace.

33/100

Automatic joy
smells like new rain on the roads
in almost summer.

34/100

The elegant swords
that made love and history
melting like spring snow.

35/100

Memories rotting
in the same painful brightness
I beg for new dreams.

36/100

Summers that throw rocks
and my distance from the stars
is still in music.

37/100

Rose petals and smiles
silently fall through the fog
that hides my seasons.

38/100

Let us go home now
to heal our platinum wounds
while the sky gets real.

39/100

Sun in the frozen
from behind the waterfall
I will dream of you.

40/100

Leaves on leaves on leaves
Verdun of blossoms as bombs
but it's spring, baby.

41/100

Just one smile away
from the most crowded darkness
I see you in me.

42/100

Degeneration
of a splendidly painful
yet forgotten spring.

43/100

Like flies on a train
that don't know about Einstein:
genesis of void.

44/100

The rainbows are back
wonderfully slaughtering
my best autumn sky.

45/100

We all will be made
of happily lost atoms
in the same blank now.

46/100

Theory of losses:
a sea of suspended leaves
craving for deserts.

47/100

Before better nights
when the world was the matter
roses hated love.

48/100

Raindrops on the beach
brave enough not to be scared
by what we all love.

49/100

Silence that explodes
over shiny new trenches
in the summer war.

50/100

There is too much light
in the sharp words we whisper
to the falling snow.

51/100

With all those mirrors
people still look for monsters
from anywhere else.

52/100

Artificial dawns
we can’t unsubscribe from
and it’s too late.

53/100

Birds of innocence
overshadowing spacetime
in my smallest dreams.

54/100

In puddles I look
at my original face
before I was born.

55/100

We counted the storms
hand in hand under tables
that made our summer.

56/100

Cities like forests
in much wetter dreams than mine
between crowns and clouds.

57/100

Infinite portraits
tessellate the robust walls
of all my scarred truths.

58/100

We cling to the rain
too afraid to realise
not all seasons die.

59/100

Atonic feelings
barefooted on frozen leaves
before a new past.

60/100

I look at each moon
wondering so stubbornly
if it will be back.

61/100

The raw silent air
over fat Shiba Inus:
more than memories.

62/100

Setting up planets
from the essential boredom
of my finest hours.

63/100

As splinted as usual
with mathematical tears
soothing my winters.

64/100

Your lasting smile
the smell of seventy seas
to call it a day.

65/100

Event horizons
in notes and neon bus stops
attiring my skin.

66/100

You running downstairs
joy of used hugs and kisses:
a rotting countdown.

67/100

Nothing but glassed love
like swimming in dark waters
in a long summer.

68/100

In the greenest void
we are all trajectories
that collide with joy.

69/100

Life as a sequence
of perfectly failing plans
to see more new moons.

70/100

Torturing my odds
in very worn golden boots
on the road to June.

71/100

War in the garden
rhetorical butterflies
on blood red roses.

72/100

Nobody could see
my soundlessly sturdy love
for your standard self.

73/100

We sit on all cliffs
seeking for accomplished stars
and a second grace.

74/100

No raincoat for me
growing happier in a storm
I wish I could stop.

75/100

Binary flowers
dooming and dominating
our daily background.

76/100

The winds are now sure
a frolic war would follow
that skeptical void.

77/100

And my only mind
is hunting in slow motion
for new sea storm friends.

78/100

Inviolated sight
of councils of verticals
dreaming of blue.

79/100

The rule of flowers
in a night walking city
one shot at a time.

80/100

Fractals of wisdom:
clouds forget very quickly
the shape of our years.

81/100

Sounds made of paper
from those very long shadows
in a deep green sky.

82/100

Reaching a goodbye
between two of your smiles
and the rest is night.

83/100

All happy people
in invisible towers:
clueless December.

84/100

Requiem for a nose
under the well tipped sunsets
sinking in poetry.

85/100

Much more drunk than you
I never stopped waiting for
the rainy season.

86/100

Baroque turning
of what could be easily killed
by staff-only seas.

87/100

Divergent white walls
excruciated afternoons
of flies not flying.

88/100

Fragile enemies
distressing lives of coral
I mainly dreamt of.

89/100

Blues to spy over
through unfamiliar curtains:
a life in four acts.

90/100

Rekindling the light
that was to slip our dry storms
we often called love.

91/100

Friends and my mountains
presumption of memories
too hard or too close.

92/100

Trees in a corner
and the revolting beauty
of a controlled sky.

93/100

We are all too warm
to be just parallel lines
in a summer dream.

94/100

Petrified tempests
scratch the light off my eyes:
past, obvious, future.

95/100

The first and the last
in my combat rain bundle
tampering with spring.

96/100

Still eyes will see
more enemies at the gate
and it's only May.

97/100

At the very edge
of each and all the best dreams
there is a mirror.

98/100

Be somewhere you love
and nothing can be harder
than obvious sunsets.

99/100

Swollen and untouched
life and deaths of my own world
of Japanese voids.

100/100

Where will you hide, boy,
when the revolution comes
to your striving heart?

Biography

Massimo Papini was born in a little Italian city more than thirty years ago.

A pianist and a very disappointed mathematician, he fell in love with any form of precise beauty while on a self-exile in Norway.

After studying Design in Italy and Glasgow he felt the urge to move to London where he eventually failed at understanding all his lives but, at the same time, he realised that poetry, yes, poetry can heal.

Massimo is a constant traveller both inside and outside his mind. He's now living between Japan and South Korea but he's really looking forwards to seeing his cat, on his piano, again.

Imprint:
Independently published

Picture on the backpage:
Abstraction of a vertical view from a brutalist balcony
— Massimo Papini

Book design:
Emilio Patuzzo

The poems collected in this book were written from October 2017 to April 2020

ISBN:
979-86-5664-319-1

from
the
hinted
deserts
*one
hundred
very
modern
haiku
poems*

introduction
from
the
hinted
deserts
biography